Meet the Moose

Meet the Moose

LEONARD LEE RUE III
with William Owen

Illustrated with photographs by Leonard Lee Rue III

DODD, MEAD & COMPANY · NEW YORK

Library of Congress Cataloging in Publication Data

Rue, Leonard Lee.
  Meet the moose.

  Includes index.
  Summary: Text and photographs examine the physical
characteristics, range, and habits of the moose.
  1. Moose—Juvenile literature. [1. Moose] I. Owen,
William, 1942–   II. Title.
QL737.U55R84   1985   599.73'57   84-26058
ISBN 0-396-08605-5

To Ken Humphries, my accountant, but more than that, my friend and advisor—L.L.R.

To my brother David whose disciplined life in the Alaskan wilderness is an inspiration and an exciting wonder—W.O.

Contents

Leonard Lee Rue III with locked moose antlers

Preface

I have photographed moose in all of their natural ranges throughout North America for thirty years, from Maine to British Columbia, from Wyoming to Labrador, and up in Alaska. I guided wilderness canoe trips into the Canadian bush country for seventeen summers before the logging industry caused a change in its incredible animal distribution. I've spent five summers in Alaska and some years I have averaged three trips per year to Rocky Mountain states in the U.S. to film moose, and I have made additional trips into other areas of moose country.

On these trips I have observed thousands of moose and I have taken thousands of photographs of these magnificent mammals. Through observation I have learned a great deal about the moose, their habits, their habitat, their requirements, and their temperaments. I hope to share this acquired knowledge and my insights with you in this book.

Two thoughts that I want to share with you are that moose impress me and have my complete respect. When I hear people talk of moose standing around like a bunch of cows, I wonder where they find such animals. You can often walk up to moose in national parks, but not in the wild! I have on rare occasion gotten close to moose in the wild with no effort on my part, but far more often I haven't even gotten a good look at them before they have gone crashing off as if they were late for an appointment.

I respect the moose because of its size. A large Alaskan bull moose will stand 7½ feet high at the shoulder with its antlers reaching to 10 feet above the ground. (If you could sit on its head, you could place a basketball through the hoop with no trouble at all.) Moose weigh as much as 1,600 pounds, and average 1,300 to 1,400 pounds. That's a lot of moose! Their antlers are the largest of any member of the world's deer family. They are often six feet from tip to tip, and weigh 50 to 60 pounds. However, one pair of antlers from an Alaskan moose was recorded at 81 inches across and weighed 95 pounds.

I also respect the moose for their grace and speed. I know that they are not noted especially for either of these characteristics, but are seen as large, slow, clumsy animals by many. Yet their exceptionally long legs and huge heart and lungs enable them to run at great speeds for long distances. Moose can trot at 35 miles per hour and have been clocked galloping at 45 mph. When a moose is panicked or just doesn't care, it goes crashing off like a runaway tank, splashing water, smashing aside branches and

Young bull moose running at full speed

brush. At other times, like fog drifting through the forest, the moose just simply appears or disappears soundlessly. It is incredible that such a large animal can move so silently.

Moose are also very proficient swimmers. Jack Focht, a fellow guide, and I, both strong canoe paddlers who have traveled over 1,000 miles a summer by canoe, tried time and again to catch up to moose that were swimming. We never could catch one. They swim at about 15 miles per hour and we couldn't paddle our canoe fast enough to overtake one.

One other thought about moose before we get into the heart of the book. A person can never tell what a moose is going to do next. I realize that in general this applies to all creatures; they are individuals and their actions may vary from what is considered normal. It's just that moose seem to vary more than do most of the other creatures. The first time my son Tim worked with me photographing moose in Mount McKinley National Park in Alaska during the rutting or mating season in the latter part of September, I warned him about their unpredictability and dangerous charges, and told him to always have an escape route in mind, such as a tree to climb or a downed tree to roll under. We were circling a willow patch where a bull moose was feeding, in order to get the sun at our backs for better pictures. Suddenly the bull charged two other photographers. One went under a fallen tree and the other up a tree. Two humans were down and the next in line were Tim and me, and the bull was only 150 feet away. We shinnied up trees in a hurry and the bull left us alone. However, Tim was impressed with this lesson.

I have certainly learned to respect and admire this huge rugged creature that has become a symbol of our northern wilds. For over thirty years the moose has been a formidable subject for my camera, and my hope is that as you learn about this magnificent creature he will afford you just as many years of future pleasure. With proper management, moose should be able to survive indefinitely in our remote and protected northern and Rocky Mountain forests.

1

Meet the Moose

The moose is not a graceful-looking animal. In fact, it looks as if it might be a combination of different animals. However, its strength is immediately apparent. A large bull—a male moose—may stand 6½ to 7½ feet at the shoulder, measure 8 to 10 feet in length from the tip of the nose to the tail, and weigh in the vicinity of 1,300 to 1,400 pounds. Weights up to 1,800 pounds have been noted. No wonder large athletes are often nicknamed "Moose."

The powerful forequarters—the front shoulders—of the moose taper back to the much smaller hind or rear parts, and end in a stubby three-inch tail. The hindquarters of a moose are slim and set lower than the massive humped forequarters. The effect is that the front legs are longer than the back legs. Early explorers reported that the moose often grazed by getting down on its front knees. I've seen moose graze on their knees, but not often.

13

A large bull moose stands about seven feet tall at the shoulder.

The moose's long legs keep its belly 36 to 40 inches off the ground and enable it to wade in fairly deep water in search of edible water plants. Those long legs also keep it from getting bogged down in deep snow.

The ears of a moose are larger than those of a mule,

14

Note the ears on this cow moose. A moose's hearing is keen.

and are independently mobile. In other words, they can
turn different ways—one to the right and the other to the
left—at the same time. This is characteristic of deer, moose,
and elk. Moose rely on their hearing and an "early warn-
ing system" of approaching danger just as our military

A moose's upper lip is flexible and used for pulling twigs into its mouth.

does on radar. I've observed moose feeding with all but their ears underwater and watched their ears twitch about like radar scanners searching for unfamiliar sounds.

The moose's face ends in a wide, flexible, down-turned muzzle. The nose and the upper lip overhang the lower lip. A short, heavy neck with a mane of long, dark hair down the back of it supports this large head. The eyes are relatively small, compared to the rest of its bulk, and its eyesight is not noted for being the best. But the nose is large and pendulous, and its sense of smell is keen. Its upper lip is extremely flexible and muscular. It is used for pulling food into its mouth.

Beneath the neck of both the male and female hangs a flap of skin, called a bell or pendant, which serves no apparent purpose. The bell will vary in size and shape. I have seen many different kinds. They are sometimes flat and sometimes round. The bell can hang from the jaw or form a long bladelike dewlap running lengthwise on the neck. The bells are usually 8 to 10 inches long, but I have seen them over two feet in length and one was reported to be 38 inches long on a cow moose. Although both cows and bulls have bells, I've found that they are more prevalent among the males. One interesting fact that no one can explain is that the bell tends to shorten as the moose ages.

Moose have magnificent antlers. They begin from the moose's forehead just above the eyes. A mature male has huge palmate antlers with small prongs projecting from the borders. They look like giant upturned hands with

The bell, or pendant, seemingly serves no purpose, but both cows (below) and bulls have them.

A moose's antlers are palmate—small prongs projecting like fingers.

many sharp fingers. Although some cows may have antlers, it is usually due to a hormone imbalance. Antlers are found normally only on the male. They can measure six feet across the widest spread and weigh up to 90 pounds, although the average weight is 50 to 60 pounds.

A mature moose has 32 teeth, 12 in the upper jaw and 20 in the lower jaw. There are no incisors or canine teeth in the upper jaw, as are found in carnivorous mammals—those that eat flesh. Each side has three premolars and three molars. The lower jaw has the same number of molars and premolars and, in addition, three incisors and one canine tooth on each side. They develop these permanent teeth by about 19 months of age. The teeth are used mainly for grinding vegetation, and the strong jaws and incisors enable the moose to bite through branches up to one-half inch in diameter. The Algonquin Indians called the moose *musee,* which means "twig eater." The early white explorers used this name and through their misunderstanding and spelling it became "moose."

I've mentioned the moose's long legs that enable it to wade through deep water and snow. They also permit it to reach high for food and to travel swiftly through tangles of fallen trees. The moose, a member of the deer family, is *unguligrade,* meaning it walks on hoofs. It has cloven hoofs, split down the middle. The moose has four toes on each foot, each encased in the horny sheath of the hoof. The two hind toes, or dewclaws, are longer than those of most members of the deer family. The moose frequents swampy, boggy areas, and when the hind toes are splayed, or spread out, the feet can more easily support the moose's weight on soft terrain.

The hair of a moose is coarse and brittle because each hair is filled with air cells, providing excellent insulation against the extremes of cold weather that the moose encounters. The moose also has a stiff mane of hair about ten inches long down the center of its shoulders. When the moose is alarmed or enraged, this mane, or roach, stands on end.

There are two other signals that a moose uses before a

Close-up of the right forefoot of a moose. Note the hind toes, or dewclaws.

Moose have a stiff mane of hair down the shoulders. Usually it is not apparent unless the moose is alarmed or enraged.

charge. Usually one occurs before the mane goes up and one after. I know, because I've seen the signs so many times. First, the ears go back, then the mane goes up, and third, the mouth opens and the tongue comes out.

I was photographing two 1½-year-old cows at Horseshoe Lake in McKinley National Park and was following them at a distance of 50 feet. One stopped to feed and the other went on. Suddenly all three signs were shown at the same time as the feeding cow turned to charge me. The closest tree was 30 feet away and I knew I'd never make it. So I threatened to throw my camera at her as she

22

charged and she veered off the trail and away from me. Thank goodness she didn't keep coming because the camera couldn't have stopped her, and besides it was my Hasselbad and worth $1800.

Moose do not have metatarsal scent glands that are so prominent in deer and found on the foot. They do have the lachrymal, or tear, gland in front of the eye. Its mildly antiseptic secretions keep the eye moist. The small tarsal glands inside the ankle are a means of communication, but I've never seen the moose use these glands as I've seen them used by deer.

The moose's dominant color is black, although it ranges through all the shades of dark brown and russet. The moose's nostrils, eye circle, inner parts of the ear, and the lower portions of its legs are grayish white.

Albinos (all white) are rare among moose, but one was killed by a Canadian trapper and mounted by John Hansen of the American Museum of Natural History. Outdoor writer and photographer Lee Wulff photographed a mutation in Newfoundland that was all white except for a hand-size patch of brown and brown eyes. Since moose are black, melanism (all black), if it occurred, would not be noticed.

It is difficult to believe that something as huge as a moose could hide anywhere. Yet nature has provided even this large mammal with a camouflage that makes it difficult to spot unless it is out in the open. Its coloration blends in amazingly well with the shadowy forest in which it lives.

At a distance, the moose is an ungainly black animal with light-colored legs. At close range, the black, or brownish black, is mostly on the breast, shoulders, and flanks, shading into rusty brown on the withers, back, neck, and head. The belly is lighter and the insides of the ears are whitish. From the knees down, the legs are a pale, warm gray. This coloring serves as a most effective camouflage in the forest.

The moose's sense of smell is highly developed, and its hearing is exceptional. However, its vision is poor and it does not seem to see stationary objects as dangerous. Often when advancing on a moose, I have frozen in my tracks every time the moose looked in my direction. Generally the animal would stare at me uncomprehendingly and then resume its feeding. This characteristic, which is true of many of the deer family, allowed me to move in quite close for my pictures—something, however, I would not advise the amateur photographer to try. When a person is as close as 10 to 20 feet, the moose's behavior can be very erratic and there's little protection against such a large animal when it decides to check you out. I always try to stay within easy reach of a tall tree to climb or a large fallen tree to roll under.

The moose can detect slight movements, but for identification and warnings it relies first upon its hearing, then upon its sense of smell for final confirmation.

2

Moose Antlers

The antlers of mature moose are truly magnificent structures of pure bone that are shed and regrown each year. Normally, only the males have antlers. Occasionally, females with antlers have been seen, but I have never seen one.

Antler growth begins early in April when a young bull moose is almost a year old, but it is not noticeable until the latter part of the month. Development is from two projections of the frontal bone known as *pedicles*, which are midway between the eyes and the ears. The antlers grow almost at right angles to the head and then sweep upward.

Antlers first appear as mere swellings, but soon develop into velvet-covered knobs. This "velvet" is soft skin with fine hairs which cover the bony material of the growing antlers and carries a network of blood vessels that provides nourishment for them.

Early stages of antler growth—at first, just knobs, then development into velvet-covered prongs. New antlers are grown each year.

Bull moose with antlers in velvet

In late August or early September, the velvet begins to peel off, leaving rigid, polished antlers.

During May and June the antlers progress rapidly and by mid-July they are about two-thirds grown. During the early stages, antlers are easily damaged, and such injuries can cause deformities. If the pedicle is damaged, the deformity recurs with each new set of antlers.

When antler development is complete, *ossification*—or hardening—begins at the base and progresses upward until the entire antler becomes rigid and hard. At this time—in late August or early September—the velvet starts to dry and peel off. The moose helps the process along

28

Bull moose with velvet peeling off antlers

Moose help discard the peeling velvet by rubbing their antlers against brush and trees.

by rubbing his antlers against trees and bushes. Some blood remains in the drying velvet, and stains may appear. The uncovered antlers are almost white at first, but continual rubbing against trees and brush stains them and produces a polished tan, which gradually changes to a dark brown. The points remain polished and white, however.

Antler growth is accomplished in about four months and is a truly remarkable phenomenon. The antlers of a mature Alaskan bull moose can weigh from 60 to 85 pounds and exceed six feet in width. Antlers are the most rapidly growing bones of mammals.

The main function of antlers appears to be related to sexual selection. When mating season begins, bugling calls

Bark has been scaled off this pine by moose antlers.

announce the presence of male moose to rival bulls, their headgear serving as a symbol of strength. When challenged by a male with smaller antlers, the stronger bulls easily chase off the younger ones.

Antlers are used in fights between the rival males for desirable females. But head-to-head combat rarely ends in serious battle or injury, since the weaker animals yield to the stronger bulls. During the fall, when the antlers are in prime condition, they may also be used against other animals, but normally the sharp hoofs of both male and female moose are their primary weapons. Once in a while, bull moose attack one another in fighting for a desired female and their antlers interlock in a permanent death-lock.

Antler shedding generally begins during the last half of December. Healthy, mature moose shed first, and the antlers are usually dropped by early January. Younger bulls shed later—two-year-olds in April, for example—but they drop their antlers earlier each year until they reach maturity.

The bull calf may develop horn "buttons" with caps on them that are visible above the hair. During the latter part of his first winter they are rubbed off.

At about sixteen months of age a young bull wears his first antlers. They are six to ten inches long and may be spiked, forked, or flattened. The size and shape show considerable variation among individuals. The following year the antlers are longer and develop prongs on either side. The third set of antlers, which mature when the

The main use of antlers is for fighting rivals during the breeding season. Here two bull moose are sparring.

moose is about forty months old, show some palmation. That is, they begin to resemble the palm of a hand with the fingers outspread. As the antlers mature, the space between the prongs fills in. The four-year-old male displays the typical adult antler form, but it is rather small.

Antlers continue to develop and grow larger each year

until the animal reaches his prime, at around six or seven years of age. The best-developed antlers come from bulls between the ages of six and twelve years. After that, antler growth tends to get smaller. The antlers of males past their prime may weigh less but have a beam larger than that of younger animals. They are also apt to be less symmetrical.

Very old moose develop antlers with few points and little palmation. Development of antlers of optimum size requires optimum conditions—adequate food supply, high mineral content of the soil, and inherited characteristics.

3

Range Today

Moose are found from coast to coast in the forested portions of Canada and the far northern forests of the United States. At one time they were plentiful, and there are still significant numbers of moose in Maine, northeastern Minnesota, Michigan around the Isle Royale region, western Montana, northern Idaho, western Wyoming, most of Alaska except the extreme west and north, and all across the wooded areas of Canada. They are not found along the Pacific coast west of the Rocky Mountains nor on the islands off the Alaskan and Canadian Pacific coasts. Both Nova Scotia and Newfoundland have moose, having been introduced into Newfoundland in 1904.

When the early explorers came to North America, moose were found as far south as Pennsylvania and even Virginia. They were hunted to extinction in their southern locales and to near-extinction in their northern locales. Loss of habitat also accounted for fewer moose along the

Distribution of moose in North America. The shaded area running down into the United States is the Rocky Mountains.

Atlantic seaboard. By the 1880s, they had vanished throughout New York and southern New England.

After many years of management and protection, moose have extended their range. The moose population in Maine has grown so much that it has spilled over into neighboring states to the extent that Vermont and New Hampshire are considering having a moose hunting season. Moose

36

have also been sighted in New York State, Massachusetts, and Connecticut. Part of the increase in the number of moose in New England is due to logging operations. Lumber companies began cutting down wide areas of forest, and without the large evergreen trees to block the sunlight, poplars, willows, and birches quickly sprouted and grew. This is moose food and moose began making a comeback.

The North American moose and the European elk are closely related and belong to the same genus, *Alces*. However, early European explorers mistakenly applied the name "elk" to the American wapiti, a large deer, instead of to the moose. The French first called the moose *l'original*. It was also known by its Indian name of *musee*, meaning "twig eater."

Both the North American moose and the European elk are called *Alces alces*, although some prefer to distinguish the American moose as *Alces americana*. The moose belongs to the mammal order Artiodactyla, which designates even-toed mammals. Its family is Cervidae, which includes all deer. There are seven subspecies of moose, and four of these are found only in North America. There is one in Europe and two in Asia. The American moose is much larger than its European and Asian cousins. In fact, it is the largest member of the deer family in the world, and the Alaskan moose (*Alces alces gigas*) is the largest of all.

Moose seem to need the harsh weather patterns of the high and northern country and most probably the vegetation that such weather allows and encourages. The moose

does not migrate in the same sense as do caribou or birds that travel over great distances between winter and summer feeding grounds or breeding and birthing grounds. It is primarily a homebody, content to remain within a fairly small area as long as there is food available.

Moose have home ranges, but they do not mark and guard them against other members of the species as some animals do. Their home range is where they feed, and moose simply go where food is plentiful. Ranges may overlap, and it is not unusual to see many moose feeding in the same area.

It has been estimated that a moose will need a browsing range of three to four square miles in order to obtain enough food. This, of course, depends on the availability of food. In the lake country of Quebec, the moose stay in the same area year round. In Alaska, moose stray to higher elevations in the summer. On the Kenai Peninsula of Alaska, which is famous for its moose, a lot of cows and calves are found along the rivers during summer, but no bulls. The bulls band together and go up into the mountainsides in summer, coming back to the thickets and swamps with the coming of the breeding season in the fall. This is also true in Mount McKinley National Park in Alaska.

During the breeding season a bull may travel miles from his home range in search of a receptive cow. But during the rest of the year it is food that determines where and

The American moose is larger than the European elk.

how far a moose will roam. Moose live in the evergreen forests of the north, but do not favor the dense mature growth. Their preference is for open places where logging or fire has destroyed the old trees and secondary growths have produced an abundance of moose food. In 1883, there was a great forest fire that wiped out thousands of acres of forest on the Kenai Peninsula. As the area began to recover with the growth of shrubs and saplings, the moose moved in and thrived. Their population exploded with the surplus of food that was available.

It is impossible to obtain an accurate census of moose or of many wide-ranging wildlife species. It is easier to report whether the species is increasing or decreasing. In 1976, the U.S. Fish and Wildlife Service estimated moose numbers in North America to range between 0.8 and 1.2 million animals.

4
Eating Habits

The moose is herbivorous. It eats only plant life and never meat. Moose are browsing animals and prefer to feed on brushy twigs. In areas where it is found, dwarf willow seems to be the favored food. In forested areas, balsam fir, white birch, and aspen are the main foods. In the summer, when moose are in lakes to escape the heat and insects, they feed heavily upon water lilies, pond weeds, sedges, and eelgrass. Alder, mountain ash, red osier, striped maple, honeysuckle, chokecherry, snowberry, spirea, dwarf birch, current, cottonwood, cranberry, and elder are high on the list of preferred foods.

Moose often eat many other foods, not through preference but because the plants may be plentiful. If all types are equally distributed, the moose will feed mainly on those listed above.

We know what moose eat by observing them while they feed and also by examining moose droppings. A full-grown moose will consume 40 to 50 pounds of food a day in winter, and 50 to 60 pounds a day in summer. The larger amount in summer is believed to represent the additional moisture in the more leafy summer browse. This is between 1,200 and 1,800 pounds a month, which is more than the average moose weighs. This can be compared to a white-tailed deer that weighs 150 pounds and eats 10 to 12 pounds of food a day, or an elk at 800 pounds and consuming only 21 pounds of food a day. The difference is not in the percentage of weight consumed daily, but the bulk amount of food needed to support the moose. Five deer can live on the same amount of browse that could support only one moose.

Because of its long legs and comparatively short neck, the moose often must get down on its knees to graze upon grasses or to drink from a shallow spring hole. Moose browse, graze, or feed for anywhere from thirty minutes to an hour at a time, although I have seen bull moose feed nonstop for over $1\frac{1}{2}$ hours.

The moose's great size is a decided asset in getting food. By merely stretching its neck upwards, it has no trouble securing food ten feet above the ground. In places where the growth is higher, the moose will rear upright, straddle the bush or sapling with its legs, force it to the ground with its body, and eat the top branches. The moose is the only member of the deer family that I have ever seen use this ingenious way of securing food. In the winter I have watched them peel long strips of bark from trees with their teeth, gouging out chunks with their lower teeth,

Bull moose feeding

which must do the job because a moose has no upper incisor teeth. Occasionally in aspen stands where moose are plentiful, bark scars, which turn black as they heal, form a visible horizontal line at moose-head height along the edge of a mountain meadow. Bark, however, is by no means a preferred item of diet.

There is no strict feeding routine. The moose may feed

at night as well as by day. Normally, when food is plentiful, as in summer and fall, there are two periods of heaviest daytime activity—before dawn to a couple of hours after, and again late in the afternoon. These are the times I am sure to observe a moose for photographing. If you are observing moose you will find them at these times in the opening along a lake shore or a forest-edge feeding ground. When their paunch is full, they retire to a thicket to drowse and chew their cud.

The moose crops its food and swallows it rapidly, chewing it only enough to swallow it. This food goes into the first of four stomach compartments. From here it is returned to the mouth in amounts the animal can chew. At this point the food is a pulp we call a cud. When it has been thoroughly rechewed, it is swallowed again and goes into the third and fourth stomach compartments where it is acted upon to provide the nourishment the moose needs to live.

June is the peak period for insects, and in order to get relief from them most of the moose retire to the rivers and lakes where they will sometimes stand completely submerged, poking their nose out just long enough to get air. At such times, eelgrass, yellow and white water lilies, sedges, and arrowleaf form the bulk of their diet. When feeding in the water, escaping the heat and insects, they will eat floating plants, or will submerge their heads to grasp mouthfuls of underwater plants. On occasion I have seen a moose dive completely beneath the surface of the water to feed on aquatic plants.

44

Cow moose feeding on underwater plants

When undisturbed and food is plentiful, moose move about very little, leaving their feeding places only to drink. Some individuals remain in the same clump of willows for as long as two weeks. They move slowly through the brush, covering only a few yards during a feeding period of 30 minutes to 1½ hours.

Mature bulls have preferred feeding areas. They move to a feeding place, sampling plants as they travel, but concentrating on one feeding spot for a long period of time.

Yearling calves lack the alertness of older animals and are often noisy in their movements. By the end of the summer they have become more independent and concentrate more on their feeding. This is good because they'll need the extra body weight for the winter months.

Cows with calves are the most alert of all and frequently assume an attentive position while chewing or swallowing just-gathered food. Their feeding periods average several hours if food is plentiful. It takes quite a long time to stow away the amount of food needed to support an adult moose. When cows feed on aquatic plants, their calves browse along the shore opposite the feeding cows in the water. When a bit older, the calves will join their mothers in feeding on plants in the water.

Like other plant eaters, moose are attracted to salt licks. This may be misleading because the common table variety of salt, sodium chloride, which is thought of when the term "salt lick" is used, may not be the essential ingredient. Other mineral compounds are found in these licks

Cow moose and calf feeding

which may be the important ones for the moose. It is probably more appropriate to call them mineral licks. Licks are most popular in the late spring and early summer and are seldom used in winter.

Mineral licks can be either earth with a high mineral content or mineral springs. Springs often become little more than trampled mud holes. Dry licks are eaten away by moose eager for the mineral salts. The moose literally *eat* the dirt. One lick in Alaska was an extensive patch of bare earth that had been eaten down several feet.

When a moose has satisfied its appetite, it will look for a resting place to "bed." In the summer it will bed in the shade and in winter, in the sun or out of the wind. The bed is created by the weight of the moose's body. Moose beds are recognizable by their shape and odor, which has been described as a combination of lysol, iodoform, and barnyard. It is thought that this smell results from waste matter excreted in the bedding area or the decomposition of urine, or both. The odor doesn't seem to bother the

A moose bed in tall grass

A huge bull moose sleeping

moose, who will return again and again to a favorite bedding place. Some, in very hot weather, will lie in a marsh
in a foot or more of water. I was surprised on my first trip
to Alaska to see how moose frequented the high country
away from water, rather than the marsh as they do in the
East. In winter moose seek beds in new, soft snow for the
insulation it affords. They'll make a new bed each night
so that the snow envelops them. Snow is, in a large part,
air and the air trapped in snowflakes acts as insulation
against severely cold temperatures.

5

From Birth to Old Age

The breeding season for moose, which lasts six weeks, peaks near the end of September through the first week in October. This season is called "the rut" and during it the bull moose becomes very belligerent and has been known to attack all sorts of things—things such as cars, trucks, a bulldozer, and trains. The moose never entirely wins such an encounter, but then the vehicle doesn't either.

Bulls that have fed together peacefully all summer now become enemies. This is because they are competing for the same cows, and breeding takes priority over all other factors. Bulls of the same group have usually determined dominance long before the rutting season begins. It is not only the strength and size of the bull that decides who the leader is, but also the size of the antlers. The larger the antlers, the higher that moose rates in the group.

I discovered this while trying to photograph moose in

A cow and bull moose during the breeding season

Wyoming. A prime bull with small antlers would not get out into the sunshine of the open meadow for a good shot. He insisted on staying in the long shadows created by the trees growing on the top of a fairly steep bank. I shouted, I whistled, I rolled small rocks down the hill. The moose couldn't have cared less. He knew I was a human and he knew he was safe from humans in the refuge. In desperation, to get him to move out into the sunlight, I picked up and carried on my shoulder a seven-foot piece of hollowed-out tree stump. I was sure that rolling that down the hill would move the moose out into the sunlight. As I topped the crest of the bank I turned

51

my body so that the big log was parallel to the hill and would roll down. About the time I turned sideways, the moose looked up at what he must have thought was the world's largest moose antlers. I not only moved that moose out of the shade, I moved him right out of the meadow. The meadow was about a half mile wide and that moose never stopped to look back once. For all I know, he may still be going.

Two strange bulls approaching one another during the rut walk with a stiff-legged gait and slowly rock their heads from side to side to make sure their opponents can see the size of their antlers. Most of the time such posturing is all that is required, with the lesser bull giving way before the larger.

When equal bulls fight, they do so with a short, sharp, savage rush, catching each other's antler thrusts with their own. Then they tear up the turf with their straining hoofs as each tries to push the other backward, seeking always for the chance to plunge their antlers into their opponent's body. They seldom get the chance, as usually most fights end with no more than one ego being crushed. The victor may chase its rival from the area and with that the fight is over.

During the rutting season, bulls search constantly for receptive cows. They travel from lake to lake, from watershed to watershed, up over ridges, hills, or mountains and down the other side. They seldom eat, they seldom sleep, they are consumed by the instinct to mate.

When a bull finds a cow, usually in her third year or

Bull moose fighting

older, that is coming into estrous (the state of being ready to breed), he will stay with her until she is ready. He will service her a number of times during a 28- to 30-hour period of fertility. He will probably stay with her for perhaps a day or two more, and then it's off again to seek out another mate. If a rival bull appears during this period, the first bull will attempt to drive him away or a fight will ensue.

The gestation period (the length of time it takes for a baby moose to develop before birth) for moose is about

245 days, with the young being born the latter part of May or the first part of June. A young cow giving birth the first time usually has a single calf. From that time on until old age, many cows will have twins.

Moose calves have a bright russet-red, unspotted coat and weigh about 25 to 35 pounds at birth. Newborn moose calves do not have the humped shoulders of the adults, nor the huge overhanging snout. The cow seeks a secluded thicket or island in a river or lake to give birth, and she and the calf stay within a small area for several weeks. She nurses her baby on through the summer.

Calves utter low bleats and are able to run swiftly when only a few days old. Soon they swim with their mother, getting a free ride when they tire by laying their heads across their mothers' backs and letting her do the legwork.

After the first several weeks close to the birthplace, calves go wherever the cow goes, staying near her from then on through the summer, fall, and winter, until it comes time to be driven off into the wilderness world on their own.

There are experts who claim that a cow moose with a calf is more unpredictable and more dangerous than the male. I won't argue that point. Anything, predator or man, that molests a moose calf is in trouble. An angered mother moose fears nothing and with her ears laid back, her mane erected, and her jaws opened wide, she charges into battle. Her powerful, slashing forefeet could kill any opponent.

In 1966, I was photographing Dall sheep in Alaska's McKinley National Park. I was about 5,500 feet up on

Cow moose and twin calves. After the first birth, a cow usually has twins.

Cabin Peak. To my amazement, I watched a cow moose lead her wobbly-legged calf up over the top of the barren peak another 500 feet or so higher than the sheep. This female had chosen the highest ridge in the area to protect her baby from the grizzly bears that patrolled the lower slopes and the banks of the river below.

A moose calf will stay with its mother through the first winter and into the following spring. During this time the cow has protected the calf and taught it how to survive.

Two weeks or so before the cow is to give birth again, she will turn on the calf and drive it away. She will run at it, threaten it, or actually strike it with her front hoofs.

As you can imagine, this sudden change in treatment from the mother confuses the calf. The calf will usually try to stay with the mother. However, after many rejections, the calf (known as a yearling because it is almost a year old) learns to keep a safe distance from its mother.

The yearling now has to decide for itself when and what to eat, where and for how long to sleep, and when to move. I have seen yearlings hang around the mother and her new calf most of the summer. But most leave and exist alone or associate with other moose. They will either group with other yearlings, or the young males with an older bull. The older bulls seem to tolerate this natural attraction of yearlings to the leadership of mature animals.

The yearling chased off by its mother to begin life all on its own is possibly now more vulnerable than at any other time to large predators and to accidental death. Often yearlings are not wary enough of what is dangerous to show fear. Soon they begin to catch on. During this year the male has its first antler-growing experience. These antlers aren't much. Usually they are simply spikes a few inches long.

At two years of age the young bull pursuing a normal antler-growth pattern has flattened forks. The next year

A moose calf must quickly learn to be alert. When a yearling, it begins life on its own.

his antlers begin to show the first real palmation, or branching, but the palms are narrow, small, and with few points. Each year thereafter, if good health continues and the seasons are favorable with a good food supply, the antlers are larger and larger. At six years of age a bull is fully mature and in his prime. However, he may continue to produce still larger, heavier antlers for six years or more, after which, in declining old age, the antlers get smaller. A moose can live to be 15 to 20 years old.

The female cow is able to mate and bear calves by the second year, but usually does not mate until the third year and every year thereafter. Young bulls are probably capable of breeding at sixteen months, but are denied the opportunity by the larger adult bulls.

6

Moose in Winter

Winter comes early and stays late in moose country. It brings bitter cold and oftentimes very deep snow. Only the healthiest moose can stand the stern test of winter and survive.

Unusually severe winters occasionally have a disastrous effect upon a moose population. This is especially true when a summer has been exceptionally dry or cool, and plant growth thus has been inhibited. As winter wears on, food becomes more and more scarce and snow piles up deeper and deeper. As the food supply dwindles and getting to it becomes more and more difficult, fat put on earlier is burned up in the continuous battle against below-zero temperatures. Starvation is a real threat, and does at times literally wipe out a local moose population.

In an ever-weakening condition, animals are susceptible to numerous diseases, such as pneumonia, and to internal parasites. As the animals lose strength, enemies become

a greater danger. Weakened moose are much easier kills for wolves.

It takes a lot of snow for a moose to flounder and get stuck so it can't move, but it does happen. Ordinarily, a moose's long legs will keep it from getting bogged down in deep snow. But the moose's ability to move through snow depends to a great extent on the depth, density, and hardness of the snow. In chest-high snow, a moose must either bound or plow through it, both of which actions may lose the animals more than they gain. The calories burned up to reach a food supply may be greater than those supplied by the food consumed.

Cows have the greatest responsibility through the winter. The safety and well-being of at least three animals depends on a single cow. She must take care of herself first, as well as her six-month-old calf which, though fairly large, is still dependent on her. An orphaned moose rarely survives the winter because unrelated cows show no inclination to protect a motherless calf. A cow that is pregnant also carries next spring's calf whose health at birth is largely determined by the mother's winter feed. A pregnant cow can become so weakened that her calves may be born prematurely or may be stillborn or born as weaklings unable to survive.

Snow is a very important factor in a moose's life. Soft snow of about 24 to 30 inches deep helps them survive.

It takes a lot of snow for a moose to get bogged down in it.

Snow of that depth does not hamper the moose's movements, and when the moose lies down, it provides insulation for the moose's body. Although the air temperature may be 50° below zero, the moose's body, protected by the soft snow, may be 25° above zero. That difference in temperature means that the moose's body will require less food to keep it warm. It is to gain this insulating blanket that the moose lies down in a different, unpacked spot of snow each time. If all the snow becomes packed down, moose will actually leave an area and seek out soft snow.

If the snow is very deep and gets a crust on it, the moose are particularly vulnerable to predators that can run across the top of the snow while the heavy moose break through and flounder about. At such times the moose often get into additional trouble because many of them will run on roads and railroads which have been cleared of snow. The trains on the Alaskan railroad between Anchorage and Fairbanks are called "moose goosers" because of the hundreds of moose that have been killed on the railroad tracks in the winter.

The presence of several animals moving from one feeding point to another in deep snows over 36 inches causes well-defined trails to be cut through the snow and creates what is known as "moose yards." These are similar to "yards" created by white-tailed deer, but moose do not use them so extensively, probably because it takes a lot more snow to immobilize a long-legged moose. Most often "yarding" is simply a natural gathering of moose on a favorable feeding ground. It is a temporary situation aris-

A bull moose browsing on willow in early spring

ing from the benefits of the food there rather than from
the desire to be social. As soon as the forage in the "yard"
becomes scarce, the group will disperse. Moose of eastern
North America show more of a tendency to "yard" than
do those in the West.

Moose paw through the snow to get at low-lying plants,
which they locate by their sense of smell. However, there
is a limit to the amount of snow they can dig through or
through which they can detect food.

The rutting season in the autumn months will leave a
bull in a weakened condition. If the weather is not too

severe in late autumn and early winter, and there is a plentiful supply of food, bulls have time to rebuild their physical condition before the severe winter weather sets in. But if heavy snows come early, many face a precarious and possibly fatal winter.

Mature bulls generally shed their antlers in late December or early January. This has some survival value because they do not have to use up energy carrying their heavy headpieces around.

Moose have no fear of ice. In fact, they prefer the ice for movement when the snow is deep because the wind will sweep the snow from the ice. It is presumed that the moose on Michigan's Isle Royale crossed over from Canada on the frozen water of Lake Superior, a distance of fifteen miles. However, sometimes moose misjudge the thickness of the ice, and break through and drown.

As winter progresses and food supplies become critical, moose eat food that does little more than fill their stomachs without providing any real nutritional value. The young tips of twigs, with bud ends and leaves, contain most of the nourishment. When shortages exist, moose consume two- and three-year-old growth with little food value. This produces malnutrition which causes losses in moose population. Just like a human, when a moose is undernourished it is subject to diseases that can kill it.

7

Moose Enemies

A healthy adult moose can stand off an attack by a pack of wolves or, if it chooses, can outrun the pack or lead it into rough, thick growth where the pack usually gives up the chase. Both wolves and moose can run at approximately 35 miles per hour, and it is usually the moose that wins.

If snow is only two feet deep, the moose has the advantage because of its long legs—unless the snow is crusted and the wolves can be supported by the crust. Then the moose is in real trouble. Moose sometimes make the mistake of fleeing across slippery ice on which they have poor footing. This is to the wolves' advantage.

Moose being killed by wolves or other predators is nature's way of assuring a strong moose population. The weak and crippled moose are the ones that are food for the wolves and therefore they do not reproduce a weak line. Studies made on Michigan's Isle Royale proved that most moose kills by wolves are of weak yearlings less than a year old or of older moose at least nine or ten years of age. This indicates that a young adult moose is in little danger of losing its life to wolves. It is just too strong. Also indicated was the fact that almost half the animals killed by wolves had one or more disabilities.

A cow protects her calf by following along behind the fleeing youngster, placing herself between it and the pack. The wolves want to separate the mother from the calf by at least 25 yards, but they are not always successful. Many wolves lose their lives in fulfilling their roles as an important ingredient in the balance of nature.

Moose are so big and strong that predators are not much of a threat to them. The smaller ones—bobcat, lynx, coyote—are of little concern, although they are capable of killing a very young calf. The effective protection provided by cows make preying on moose calves a more hazardous undertaking than these predators generally want to face. And within a few months the calf is 150 to 200 pounds and can give a good account of itself against these much smaller animals.

Wolverine are reported to kill a moose calf once in a while, but it's not very common. Cougar are capable of killing moose, but do so rarely. I do not know of a reported cougar kill of moose since 1947.

Black bears are probably little, if any, threat to adult moose. Any descriptions I've ever read of an encounter between a black bear and an adult moose ended in the death of the bear or its escape up a tree. I have viewed

Most wolf kills of moose are weak yearlings or older moose with disabilities. A young adult moose is in little danger from wolves.

them feeding in the same meadow in western Canada, with no signs of hostility between them, just a normal animal's awareness of what is near. I call it "watchful disregard."

The grizzly and big brown bear, the largest carnivores (meat eaters) in North America, are treated with a great deal more respect than the black bear by the moose. They are a greater threat. Grizzlies have killed adult moose in our eastern states when the spring snows have caused moose to flounder. In Canada grizzlies feed extensively on elk and moose, which they apparently run down and kill.

Brown bears do kill some moose, but by the time the calf is three weeks to a month old, it is strong enough to outrun the bear. The moose can also outswim a mature brown bear.

Wolves, the major moose predators, do most of their killing during the winter. In the summer their diet is mainly small game, such as beaver, rabbits, and the like. If they get a moose, it is usually a calf. This is because moose are tough opponents and can kill or cripple a wolf with a slash or kick from the front or rear hoofs.

During midwinter, when small game becomes scarce, wolves turn their attention to moose. A lone wolf can kill a weakened moose, but wolves pack up in winter and work as a team. These packs vary in size from five or six animals to 16 animals.

Starvation is probably the moose's greatest natural killer. In many areas, such as New Brunswick and Nova Scotia, the moose herds were almost wiped out because of over-protection. In both places the moose population crashed shortly after hunting was no longer pemitted. The closed season—when no one could hunt moose for one or more years—allowed the moose to increase to the point where they destroyed their food supply and starvation was inevitable.

Grizzlies have been known to kill moose.

Parasites, both internally and externally, take their toll. In the summer, life is made miserable for the moose by the clouds of stinging, biting, blood-sucking insects that prey upon them. I have seen moose whose hind legs were a scabrous mess with fly bites. Moose seek lakes to escape from both heat and insects.

In Canada where I guided for seventeen summers, the young men would ride after swimming moose in a motor boat and jump on their backs for a ride. They would immediately be covered with flies because as the moose sank lower in the water the flies from the moose's back would swarm up and the young men would literally turn black with flies.

Moose ticks sometimes infest a moose by the hundreds. In summer, with a plentiful supply of food, the moose can usually withstand the onslaught of the ticks. In winter, the ticks may be such a drain that the moose may be severely weakened. By trying to rub the ticks off, the moose will scrape off a lot of its hair. This, in turn, causes a loss of body heat, and the moose may suffer.

Moose are also subject to liver flukes, tapeworms, and other intestinal parasites. Particularly in the Northeast, a tiny worm only about as thick as a human hair is a real enemy. The worms live inside snails and slugs that cling to the forage that moose and deer eat. These parasites don't seem to bother deer, but in moose the worms get into the central nervous system and destroy brain tissue. The moose in such a condition loses all fear of man and wanders around groggily while its strength lasts. It holds its body in a humpbacked position, with its head low or cocked in an odd pose. It may even become blind. This condition is known as "moose sickness." Pathologists are still studying this disease, which is always fatal.

8

Moose and People

In early times, the moose was the mainstay of the northern Indian. It was a food source, contributing as much as 500 pounds or more of prime meat when a large bull was killed. The muzzle, or nose, was considered a great delicacy. The heavy hide furnished clothing, moccasin leather, and material for snowshoes. Little was wasted. The back sinew was used for sewing thread. The coarse, bristly mane furnished material for embroidery. The antlers and bones were made into tools. Hoofs were converted into rattles for use in religious ceremonies.

The first white men to see moose were French explorers of the early seventeenth century. However, these earliest explorers provided only sketchy descriptions of the animals they encountered and it was not until after Champlain's extensive explorations that the moose, or *l'original* as the French called it, was described and recognized as being similar to the European elk.

It didn't take the white man long to discover the value of moose. The exploitation of moose by both the white man and the Indians soon brought about a noticeable decrease in moose populations all across settled parts of eastern Canada and the northeastern United States. By 1800, the future of moose was uncertain in many parts of its range.

The westward movement of man had both a good and bad influence on moose. In the beginning it was mostly bad, due to overhunting. Later, extensive cutting of timber along with accidental and natural forest fires provided food and additional range for moose. As a rule, though, where man's presence increases, the moose's presence decreases.

Records of moose left by early explorers are far from complete, but indicate that moose were common all across

A young bull moose playfully challenges an older bull.

Bull moose climbing a riverbank

the northern states with the exception of the area west of the Continental Divide. Their movement southward apparently came in the 1860s and early 1870s when a few moose were seen in Wyoming's Yellowstone Park. By 1968 there were 700 moose wintering in the Grand Teton National Park in Wyoming.

The Indians of northern North America were well aware

of the value of the great moose, and did not neglect it in their songs and legends. They believed that dreams of moose meant a long life for the dreamer.

Though only a small percentage of Americans and Canadians have ever seen a live moose, most are familiar with the name and have at least some idea of what a moose looks like. Moose have been characterized in cartoons for years.

The bigness of the moose has caused its adoption as a word meaning "very large," and many big football players have been known as "Moose." A number of proper names incorporate the word "moose." There is the Moose River in central Ontario in Canada, Moose Jaw is a city in Saskatchewan, and Moosehead Lake is the largest lake in the state of Maine. The moose is also the official state animal of Maine.

An American fraternal organization, founded in 1888 and which has over a million members today, is called the Loyal Order of Moose. This benevolent group maintains a village for parentless children called Moose Heart in Aurora, Illinois, and a retirement village and hospital known as Moose Haven in Jacksonville, Florida.

At one time there was even a political party named after the moose. It was an offshoot of the Republican Party and was popularly called the Bull Moose Party. Its presidential candidate was Theodore Roosevelt, who was said to have named the party with a comment on his own health and fitness for the office of president. He said he felt "fit as a moose!"

74

Moose are excellent swimmers.

Today, the moose is considered a desirable species, not only for its food value but as hunters' trophies for the antlers and head. Most importantly, moose are fascinating animals that should be preserved.

The moose is such an integral part of the north country that I can't visualize it as wilderness without the moose being there. In some areas the moose population has been decimated by overhunting, but it doesn't have to be that way. With wise and proper management, the moose can always be a part of the wilderness to thrill thousands of others as it has thrilled me.

Index

LEONARD LEE RUE III has devoted his life to photographing and writing about wildlife. Today he is the most widely published wildlife photographer in North America and probably the world. His work appears in over fifty publications a month here and abroad.

His adult books include *The Deer of North America* and *Fur-bearing Animals of North America.* His most recent title for young readers was *Meet the Opossum*, done with William Owen. Rue is a former camp ranger, wilderness canoe guide, and game keeper. He lectures to school and civic groups and conducts outdoor educational and field trips.

WILLIAM OWEN, a close friend of the author, is a Presbyterian minister in Frenchtown, New Jersey. He has long been interested in wildlife and is co-author of *The Search* with Tom Brown, Jr., the story of Brown's experience as a woodsman and tracker, and of wilderness survival.